the CRUNCH WRAP

WHAT IS A CRUNCH WRAP?

Have you had the original crunch wrap at Taco Bell®? Ha! These are nothing like that. But also kind of like that. A healthy, el-evated, VARIABLE version of that. To me, what makes a crunch wrap is its shape. Instead of folding the wrap into a burrito or quesadilla, it's wrapped into a sort of pentagon (hexagon?), giving you plenty of surface area to layer all of your goodies. Add a nice, pan-fried seal and a crispy outside, and you have crunch wrap perfection. You can fill your wrap with meaty, saucy fill-ings, like you would a burrito; or fresh, layered sandwich top-pings (my favorite); or even get creative with sweet, treat-like flavors. You can use any wrap large enough to get the job done, but the low-carb flatbreads I'll mention below are IDEAL for building your large, super-satisfying wrap with KILLER macros.

WHAT KIND OF WRAP WORKS BEST?

1. **Joseph's Lavash®** work great and have excellent macros at 3f/18c/10p and 120 calories for one huge wrap. They're soft and flexible and they can be found at many Walmart® stores, as well as on Amazon®.
2. **Cut Da Carb®** wraps are my personal and absolute favorite for this. They can only be purchased on their Web site (cutdacarb.com), so they're less accessible than the Joseph's, but they win in macros, flavor, and texture for me. I do receive free wraps (and I hope they never end!), but I'm not sponsored by them, so I don't make any money if you buy them. I'm just obsessed. The flavor is so good when they're crisped up, and they do actually get crispy! The macros can't be beat at just 0.5f/14c/4p and 80 calories, and they have a nice, short, clean ingredient list.

But, in or ... the whole giant flatbread, they're SUPER thin and can be hard to work with. Some bags seem very fresh and flexible; some are more dry and brittle. It's totally worth it to me for the taste and the macros!

ANY GLUTEN-FREE OPTIONS?

I wish there were a perfect gluten-free alternative, but I've yet to find anything large enough to completey wrap up your toppings like the Cut Da Carb or Joseph's. I would suggest experimenting with your favorite gluten-free tortillas, and folding it in half like a quesadilla or into a smaller burrito or two. The magic will still happen if you pan-fry it after folding. I did this with a gluten-free BFree® Quinoa Chia Seed wrap. It was definitely smaller, but still fabulous in taste and macros! I've also heard good things about the gluten-free options from Mission®, Siete®, and Joseph's.

HOW DO YOU KEEP YOUR CUT DA CARB FROM BREAKING?

- Keep extra bags stored in the box they were delivered in (so they stay totally flat) in the freezer.

- Keep one bag sealed in your fridge, also lying flat. Don't open the bag to get your wrap until all of your fillings are prepped, weighed, and ready to go.

- Wet a paper towel and lay it over the top of your wrap for a few minutes if it is exceptionally dry (or spray with a light mist of water). You can also watch a video with these tips on the Cut-Da-Carb Web site.

- Don't overstuff! This is hard for me since I want every veggie under the sun. But remember: you can always stuff extra fresh greens in afterward.

- Wrap quickly and carefully and set seam-side down into a HOT, sprayed pan immediately. Even if your wrap has cracked, it's almost always salvaged in the pan for me!

- When it's not salvaged, just embrace the mess! It's worth it for the macros and flavor.

- Save any brittle or broken wraps to bake later as chips! You'll need some of those anyway—they're amazing.

HOW DO YOU "CRUNCH WRAP IT"

Throughout these recipes, you'll see a repeated instruction: "Crunch Wrap It." Each recipe will use essentially the same method to cook, so I thought I'd save us both the redundancy. Here's how to "Crunch Wrap It":

1. Heat a pan to medium/high heat halfway through building the wrap.

2. Move your plate (with open, topped wrap) right next to the pan for a smooth transfer.

3. Spray pan with cooking spray, THEN begin wrapping. Fold bottom right corner toward the middle, then bottom left corner, left side, right side (holding it all in gently as you go), then top left, and top right.

4. Hold the wrap together like it's a precious gem and carefully place it folded-side down onto your hot pan. Spray the top with cooking spray and sprinkle with coarse salt. Let it cook for a minute or two, until browned, crisp, and sealed.

5. Flip carefully and cook the other side for a minute. Remove from pan and slice in half, using sawing motions, with a bread knife. Eat immediately, preferably with nobody bugging you, because that's the worst.

You can find a video tutorial in the highlights of my Instagram page, @lillielovesmacros

CAN YOU USE AN AIR FRYER OR PANINI STYLE GRILL?

Lots of readers love to make these in their air fryers! I haven't tried this approach, but I'm sure it's amazing. Others love their George Foreman Grill®. I'm often doing a sandwich-style crunch wrap for lunch, and my goal is to get the outside toasty while keeping the inside pretty cool and crunchy, so I stick with the quick, direct heat from a pan. But the grill would be perfect when you want the inside super hot and melty.

HOW DO YOU KEEP THE GREENS FROM GETTING SOGGY?

First of all, this is why most of my recipes include arugula. Personally, it's my favorite green. I love the peppery flavor it adds, and in my opinion, it can handle a little wilt and still be good. (I do NOT feel the same about Romaine.) HOWEVER, I still prefer that the arugula stay fresh and cool. Here are my tips for maintaining that freshness.

1. Don't let the greens be first or last in your line-up. Sandwich them in the middle somewhere, so there are more barriers between the greens and the heat.

2. Cook your crunch wrap hot and fast, with the goal being to seal the seams and crisp up the outside. Quickly remove and slice in half, with a serrated knife, immediately.

3. You might want to cook your wrap in a pan rather than a panini press or air fryer if you're concerned about the inside getting too hot.

CAN YOU MAKE IT AHEAD TO PACK FOR LUNCH?

Some people do! You'll want to have a pan, toaster oven, air fryer, or George Foreman Grill if you're hoping to bring back any crisp. The wrap is like a toasted sandwich and will get soft if it's wrapped up for later. If you don't mind the texture, you can eat it soft and cold, or soft and microwaved. Skip the tomatoes or anything too juicy to avoid a soggy wrap—you can always stuff those ingredients in after you cut it in half to eat!

I would love it if these worked great for your meal-prep, but they are definitely best served fresh, right off the pan! If you love the flavors of a certain crunch wrap but can't properly reheat it at work, you could pack it up deconstructed. Build it as a salad with extra greens and skip the wrap. Or bake the wrap into chips ahead of time and eat them with your salad!

HOW DO YOU LOG THEM IN "MY FITNESS PAL" ?

Just like my Lillie Eats and Tells Cookbook, all of the recipes in this book have already been entered into the My Fitness Pal (MFP) database. That way, you can follow the recipe and simply search and log accordingly. Since I know we won't all have the same wraps available to us, I've entered the nutritional info for the crunch wrap "naked"—that means it does not include the flatbread. You'll log that particular "Lillie Eats and Tells Crunch Wrap Naked" along with your Cut Da Carb, or Joseph's Lavash, or whatever wrap you end up using. Maybe you don't log any wrap at all because you've packed the fillings for work as a salad! I did it this way because it's very easy to log your own wrap, but a little trickier to try and adjust the numbers when you're not using the same one as me.

With each recipe in this book, you'll see the macros *including* the Cut-Da-Carb. Don't let that confuse you. When you go to log it from MFP, you'll find a lighter set of macros (Cut-da-Carb subtracted out) since you'll be logging your own wrap in addition.

Search MFP for "Lillie Eats and Tells" (and then the exact title of the crunch wrap). Or, of course, you can always just log your own components and add/subtract whatever you like. There is no limit to what you can stuff in one of these wraps!

CAN YOU ADJUST THE MACROS IF YOU MAKE SMALL CHANGES TO YOUR CRUNCH WRAP?

If you want to change or skip a few of my ingredients, but still prefer the ease of logging the "Lillie Eats and Tells" version, you can go to MFP on YOUR DESKTOP (not phone) and enter an ingredient as a negative, which will remove those macros from your diary. For example, if you skip the 28 grams of avocado, you can log -28 grams of avocado to your diary from your desktop. Or you can leave it and figure it's no big deal. I support that too!

FLAVOR MAKERS

Some of our all-time favorite sauces and additions to take your crunch wrap to the next level. When you see these flavor makers in a recipe, reference them here!

SKINNY CHIPOTLE CREAM

1 cup fat-free sour cream
2 chipotle peppers from the can
1 Tbsp. adobo sauce from the same can

Spoon 1 cup sour cream into a small food processor or blender jar. Add about 2 chipotle peppers plus 1 Tbsp. of the sauce (depending on how much heat you like) to the sour cream and blend or process.

2 Tbsp. (30g)= 28 Cal, 0.3F, 4.5C, 1.7P

JALAPEÑO AVOCADO CAESAR DRESSING

½ cup non-fat Greek yogurt
½ cup reduced-fat buttermilk
Half an avocado (40 g)
1 oz (28 g) cotija cheese
½ tsp. onion powder
2 frozen garlic cubes (or 2 minced cloves)
¾ tsp. salt
¼ tsp. pepper
2 Tbsp. fresh lemon juice (30 g)
1/2 −1 fresh jalapeño (30 g)
Handful of cilantro (or parsley if you hate it!) (20 g)
2 green onions (10 g)

Blend all ingredients until smooth.

2 Tbsp. (30g)= 24 Cal, 1.2F, 1.2C, 1.7P

CREAMY CHIMICHURRI

1 cup fresh cilantro*
1/3 cup fresh basil leaves
1/4 cup white balsamic vinegar
Juice from half a lemon
2 cloves garlic (frozen dorot cubes)
1/2 Tbsp. olive oil
1/2 tsp. salt
1/4 tsp. pepper
Pinch of red pepper flakes
3 Tbsp. non-fat Greek yogurt

Pulse in small food processor or blender to desired consistency. We like it a little chunky. If it gets too smooth, I like to whisk in a little exra chopped cilantro.

*If you hate cilantro, use any combo of herbs you love. Basil, parsley, mint, oregano—even arugula or kale can work.

2 Tbsp. (30g) =33Cal, 1.3F,3.1C,0.9P

LIGHT BASIL GARLIC AIOLI

2 frozen Dorot® garlic cubes (or 2 cloves, minced)
2 tsp. basil paste (or 1 Tbsp. minced basil)
1/2 cup fat-free sour cream
Pinch of salt and pepper

Thaw cubes and mix in a small dish.

Reduced-fat sour cream will only add a little fat per serving. Non-fat Greek yogurt or low-fat mayo works great, too. I just prefer the consistency and mild flavor of the sour cream. If you use a different base, just log the sour cream or mayo—the other additions are nearly negligible anyway.

2 Tbsp. (30g) =27Cal, 0F, 4.8C,0.9P

LIGHTENED-UP, CREAMY CILANTRO-LIME RANCH

1 packet of ranch dressing mix (1 oz)
1 cup light mayo*
1 cup fat-free milk (add more if it's too thick)
¼ cup salsa verde
1-2 jalapeños seeded
2 cloves of garlic, minced (or frozen cubes)
1 whole lime juiced (about 2 Tbsp.)
½ cup packed cilantro

Blend all ingredients in a blender or food processor until smooth. Place in fridge for an hour if you have time. No big deal if not.

I use Best Foods® "low-fat mayonnaise dressing", with a blue label, which only has 1 gram of fat per serving for these macros. You can also use fat-free or reduced-fat sour cream, or Greek yogurt if you prefer.

2 Tbsp. (30g) = 21Cal, 0.7F, 2.8C, 0.8P

QUICK PICKLED ONIONS

1/2 cup apple cider vinegar
1 Tbsp. sugar
1.5 tsp. kosher salt
1 cup water
1 medium red onion, thinly sliced

Mix first four ingredients together in a jar and add thinly sliced onion. Let sit at room temp for 30 minutes to an hour. Store in fridge in the liquid for 7-10 days and use on everything!

Macros hardly change, so I just log raw onion.

BRUNCH WRAPS

*Filled with your favorite classic—
and not-so-classic—breakfast flavors!*

MEDITERRANEAN BREAKFAST
DRIPPY EGG B.L.A.T.
MONTE CRISTO
SCRAMBLED EGG WITH LEMONY GARLIC AIOLI
EGG WHITE AND TURKEY SAUSAGE
VEGGIE, TURKEY SCRAMBLE

MEDITERRANEAN BREAKFAST CRUNCH WRAP

When you've got leftover ground turkey in the fridge and a full day ahead, you deserve something legit-that rings in just about the same as a protein bar!

1 Cut Da Carb wrap

2 Tbsp. hummus (I use one with 2-3 fat per serving)

1.5 oz (50 g) leftover, cooked ground turkey (93/7)

4 oz (112 g) liquid egg whites

1 oz jarred roasted red peppers, chopped

Sweet bell pepper, diced (20 g)

2 tsp. fat-free feta cheese (Trader Joe's® sells some)

Arugula

1 small tomato, sliced (70 g)

Salt and pepper

Fresh basil or parsley (optional)

Search MFP for: "Lillie Eats and Tells Mediterranean Breakfast Crunch Wrap Naked." This will show you lower macros withOUT the wrap, so you can log this filling ALONG with whatever wrap you use.

Macros with the Cut Da Carb:
314 Cal, 8F, 26C, 33P, 8 Fiber

1. Heat a pan to medium heat and then spray with cooking spray.

2. Immediately add cooked ground turkey, liquid egg whites, roasted peppers, fresh bell peppers, and feta. Season to taste with salt and pepper, and gently push around the pan until just set. Try and keep it in one whole piece, like a large pancake for easier wrap-building. Flip the whole thing to make sure it's cooked on top, then transfer to a plate to cool. (Pop it in the fridge while you prep the rest.)

3. Spread the middle of your wrap with hummus.

4. Top with the ground turkey/egg mixture, arugula, tomato slices, and fresh herbs if using. Add a pinch of good salt and fresh ground pepper to your tomatoes.

5. Crunch wrap it.

DRIPPY EGG B.L.A.T. CRUNCH WRAP

Because yolks look good on everyone.

1 Cut Da Carb wrap

1.5 Tbsp. (20 g) chipotle cream (see "flavor makers")

1 fried egg + 2 fried egg whites, seasoned with salt and pepper

Romaine or iceberg lettuce

1 medium tomato, sliced thick (100 g)

1 oz (28 g) avocado, sliced

2 slices of bacon (I use Costco precooked)

Everything But the Bagel Sesame Seasoning® (I find mine at Trader Joe's or Costco®)

1. Put eggs in the fridge for just a minute after frying to cool them down a bit and avoid a soggy wrap.

2. Spread middle of wrap with chipotle cream.

3. Top with egg whites, fried egg, lettuce, tomato, avocado, and bacon. Sprinkle with Everything But the Bagel Sesame Seasoning.

4. Crunch wrap it.

Search MFP for: "Lillie Eats and Tells Drippy Egg BLAT Crunch Wrap Naked." This will show you lower macros withOUT the wrap, so you can log this filling ALONG with whatever wrap you use.

Macros with the Cut Da Carb:
352 Cal, 16F, 25C, 26P, 8 Fiber

MONTE CRISTO
BRUNCH WRAP

There's nothing like the massive ham and cheese, deep-fried Monte Cristo experience from Disneyland®, it's true. But this light little number still takes me to a happy place!

1 Cut Da Carb wrap

1 tsp. French's® honey mustard

2 egg whites

Small pinch of Stevia®

Cinnamon

2 oz (56 g) good deli ham (I like Columbus® Black Forest Ham)

2 slices (40 g) light Swiss cheese (like Jarlsberg®)

1 Tbsp. (15g) sugar-free raspberry jam (Smucker's® here for 5 carbs)

1 Tbsp. raspberries (15 g), smashed with a tiny bit of Stevia (optional)

Sprinkle of powdered sugar (3 g)

Search MFP for: "Lillie Eats and Tells Monte Cristo Crunch Wrap Naked." This will show you lower macros withOUT the wrap, so you can log this filling ALONG with whatever wrap you use.

Macros with the Cut Da Carb:
325 Cal, 9F, 26C, 36P, 7 Fiber

1. Fry the egg whites in a pan over medium heat, keeping together like a pancake. Season with a pinch of Stevia, a sprinkle of cinnamon, and a little salt. Top immediately with one slice of cheese and cover to melt.

2. Spread the middle of your wrap with honey mustard and then top with egg whites (cheese-side down against the wrap), then ham, sugar-free jam, raspberries (if adding), and extra slice of cheese.

3. Crunch wrap it. But with no fresh veggies in this one, you might want to let it cook a little longer, at a lower heat, to get the cheese nice and melty. You can brush the outside of the wrap with a little extra egg white while cooking, then sprinkle with cinnamon. Flip an extra time to get cinnamon on both sides.

4. Remove from heat, slice in half, then sprinkle with a few grams of powdered sugar. Serve with additional jam or your favorite sugar-free syrup.

SCRAMBLED EGG
BRUNCH WRAP with lemony garlic aioli

Inspired by one of the richest, most amazing breakfast sandwiches I've ever had at Devil's Teeth Baking Company® in San Francisco. It had eggs, cheese, bacon, avocado, and lemon garlic aioli on a big, fresh, golden buttery biscuit. It was a heart attack that made my heart sing. This wrap is almost nothing like it (ha!), but it still brings me back. Great for an extra low-carb meal.

1 Cut Da Carb wrap

1½ Tbsp. (20 g) skinny lemony garlic aioli (see step 1 below)

1 slice lite provolone

2 eggs + 2 whites, scrambled just till set

¼ of a small avocado (20g)

Arugula (optional)

2 slices of Canadian bacon (I get mine at Costco)

Search MFP for: "Lillie Eats and Tells Scrambled Egg Brunch Wrap Naked." This will show you lower macros withOUT the wrap, so you can log this filling ALONG with whatever wrap you use.

Macros with the Cut Da Carb:
398 Cal, 17F, 21C, 40P, 6 Fiber

1. Make lemon garlic "aioli" by stirring together a couple of Tbsps. of fat-free sour cream with 1/2 cube frozen garlic, ½ Tbsp. fresh lemon juice and a few zests of a lemon. (Non-fat Greek yogurt or reduced-fat sour cream will also work great and macros will only change slightly.)

2. Spread middle of wrap with skinny lemon garlic aioli.

3. Top with lite provolone, soft scrambled eggs (mix of eggs and whites that have been cooked and let cool a bit), avocado, Canadian bacon, and arugula.

4. Crunch wrap it.

EGG WHITE AND TURKEY SAUSAGE CRUNCH WRAP

This is my go-to when I want to keep the carbs extra low.

1 Cut Da Carb wrap

1 Spicy Pepper Jack Laughing Cow Cheese® wedge

1.5 Tbsp. (20 g) skinny chipotle cream (see flavor makers)

1 slice (21 g) reduced-fat Swiss cheese

4 egg whites, pan-fried into a flat cake and slightly cooled (125 g)

1 tomato, sliced thick (100 g)

1 Jimmy Dean® Turkey Sausage link, sliced thin or chopped

Arugula

Sliced red onion (15 g)

Diced bell pepper (20 g)

Search MFP for: "Lillie Eats and Tells Egg White and Turkey Sausage Crunch Wrap Naked." This will show you lower macros withOUT the wrap, so you can log this filling ALONG with whatever wrap you use.

Macros with the Cut Da Carb: 332 Cal, 27c, 8f, 33p, 7 fiber

1. Build wrap by spreading cheese wedge and chipotle cream in the middle of the flat wrap. Add Swiss, egg whites, tomatoes, sausage, arugula, red onion, and bell pepper.

2. Crunch wrap it. Feel free to add hot sauce or salsa.

VEGGIE, TURKEY SCRAMBLE CRUNCH WRAP

A great way to use up any leftover roasted or sautéed veggies, and a yummy, savory, filling start to the day!

1 Cut Da Carb wrap

1 Spicy Pepper Jack Laughing Cow Cheese wedge

100 g liquid egg whites

1 whole egg

1/4 cup (60 g) low-fat cottage cheese

1/4 cup (60 g) sautéed peppers and onions (leftover from fajitas!)

35 g favorite deli turkey

Small handful of arugula or spinach, chopped

A good pinch of kosher salt and twist of fresh ground pepper

1 slice reduced-fat provolone cheese

Search MFP for: "Lillie Eats and Tells Veggie, Turkey Scramble Crunch Wrap Naked." This will show you lower macros withOUT the wrap, so you can log this filling ALONG with whatever wrap you use.

Macros with the Cut Da Carb:
406 Cal, 12F, 27C, 42P, 6 Fiber

1. In a bowl, beat together egg whites, egg, and cottage cheese. Add sautéed peppers and onions (see the fajita chicken and veggies recipe on my blog [Lillieeatsandtells.com] if you need directions), chopped turkey, and a chopped arugula or spinach. Add salt and pepper and combine.

2. Heat a pan over medium heat, then spray with a mist of olive oil spray. Add egg mixture and push around the pan to cook. When it's just set, top with a slice of provolone and cover with a lid to melt. Add any additional salt and pepper to taste. Transfer eggs to a plate to cool, careful to keep them all in one piece if possible. Pop your plate in the fridge for a minute to cool so it doesn't make your wrap soggy.

3. Lay your wrap flat and spread with the cheese wedge. Top with slightly cooled eggs and crunch wrap it. Work quickly to avoid the heat and moisture of the eggs breaking the wrap.

This collection of crunch wraps uses easy, pre-cooked protein sources like deli meat, rotisserie chicken, tuna, and frozen chicken burgers. This way, you can keep your favorites stocked and whip up a delicious lunch in minutes!

LUNCH WRAPS

ZESTY TUNA SALAD
VEGGIE
TURKEY, PEAR, AND ARUGULA
ITALIAN STALLION
EASY FIG AND GOAT CHEESE CHICKEN BURGER
FRESH THAI CHICKEN
DIPPY CHICKEN PARMESAN
EASY MAHI BURGER

ZESTY TUNA SALAD CRUNCH WRAP

I love that you can make the tuna salad ahead and still get all of the vibrant veggies without starting from scratch at lunch time!

ZESTY TUNA SALAD

1 can drained albacore tuna (142g)

3 Tbsp. non-fat Greek yogurt (45 g)

1 Tbsp. French's honey mustard (15 g)

2 Tbsp. lemon juice (30 g)

1 tsp. grainy dijon mustard (5 g)

2 Tbsp. chopped pepperoncinis (30 g)

Handful of sweet bell pepper, diced (30 g)

Handful of cucumber, diced (45 g)

1-2 green onions, chopped (10 g)

Handful of diced tomato (50 g)

Half an avocado, diced (45 g)

Small handful of chopped cilantro (optional)

Pinch of salt, pepper, and red pepper flakes

ZESTY TUNA SALAD CRUNCH WRAP

1 Cut Da Carb wrap

1.5 Tbsp. (20 g) skinny chipotle cream (see "flavor makers")

1 thin slice (20 g) of good sharp white cheddar cheese (full-fat yumminess!)

140 g Lillie Eats and Tells zesty tuna salad

1 tsp. honey mustard (4 g)

Butter lettuce

Pinch of sliced red onion (15 g)

Sliced tomato (70 g)

Sliced peaches (30 g)

1. Make your tuna salad by mixing together all ingredients. This will keep in your fridge for 3-5 days.

2. Build wrap by spreading skinny chipotle cream in the center. Top with a thin slice of sharp white cheddar cheese, tuna salad, a drizzle of honey mustard, lettuce, onions, tomatoes, and peaches.

3. Crunch wrap it.

Make sure your lettuce is not added first or last but wedged in the middle to help keep it cool and crisp. Cook hot and fast! Remove from heat and cut in half with a serrated knife immediately.

Search MFP for: "Lillie Eats and Tells Zesty Tuna Salad Crunch Wrap Naked." This will show you lower macros withOUT the wrap, so you can log this filling ALONG with whatever wrap you use.

Macros with the Cut Da Carb:
330 Cal, 10F, 32C, 26P, 8 Fiber

VEGGIE CRUNCH WRAP

This is the crunch wrap I eat when I DON'T want to use up my protein since I cherish mine. If you want to add protein to this, go for it! It's great with all sorts of yummy meats added in. Low-fat or fat-free cheeses can add a decent amount of protein as well. But sometimes I just really love having room for ALL THE VEGGIES.

1 Cut Da Carb wrap

1.5 Tbsp. (22 g) hummus (I use a lower fat option that's 2.5 fat/2Tbsp.)

Baked sweet potato, peeled and sliced (40 g)

1 small tomato, sliced thick (80 g)

¼ of a pear, sliced thin (30 g)

Cucumber, sliced (30 g)

Pickled onions and/or radishes, sliced super thin (I like to pickle mine in the same liquid as my onions—see "flavor makers" for recipe)

Bell pepper, diced (20 g)

¼ of an avocado, sliced thin (28g)

1 tsp. honey mustard (4 g)

Pinch of arugula

Large pinch of cabbage or broccoli slaw

Search MFP for: "Lillie Eats and Tells Veggie Crunch Wrap Naked." This will show you lower macros withOUT the wrap, so you can log this filling ALONG with whatever wrap you use.

Macros with the Cut Da Carb:
290 Cal, 7F, 44C, 11P, 11 Fiber

1. Build wrap by spreading cheese wedge in the middle. Top with hummus; sliced, baked sweet potato; tomatoes; pear; cucumber; pickled onions and/or radishes; bell pepper; and avocado. Drizzle with honey mustard. Add a handful of arugula, and if there's still room and you've got it, a large pinch of cabbage or broccoli slaw for crunch!

2. Crunch wrap it.

TURKEY, PEAR, AND ARUGULA CRUNCH WRAP

I know it's just deli meat tucked in there, but this is my go-to, classic crunch wrap and the one I ate for nearly a year straight. Ha! There is just something about this combination that has my heart.

1 Cut Da Carb wrap

1 Spicy Pepper Jack Laughing Cow cheese wedge

1.5 Tbsp. (20 g) skinny chipotle cream (see "flavor makers")

3.5 oz turkey (100 g, but sometimes just 80 g is great for me)

1 medium tomato, sliced thick (90 g)

1.5 Tbsp. avocado, sliced thin (20 g)

Pickled onions (30 g)(see "flavor makers")

¼ of a pear, sliced thinly (30 g)

2 Tbsp. red, yellow, or orange bell pepper, diced (20 g)

2 tsp. honey mustard (8 g)

Big handful of arugula

Salt/ pepper/Trader Joe's Everything But the Bagel Sesame Seasoning

Search MFP for: "Lillie Eats and Tells Turkey, Pear, and Arugula Crunch Wrap Naked." This will show you lower macros withOUT the wrap, so you can log this filling ALONG with whatever wrap you use.

Macros with the Cut Da Carb:
360 Cal, 6F, 39C, 33P, 9 Fiber

1. Build wrap by spreading Laughing Cow wedge, chipotle cream, 50 grams of the turkey, tomatoes, avocado, pickled onions, pear, bell pepper, honey mustard, seasonings, and a big handful of arugula. Top with remaining 50 g of turkey. This protects the arugula from getting too wilty.

2. Crunch wrap it.

ITALIAN STALLION CRUNCH WRAP

Your extra-light Italian sub! Pictures don't do this guy justice.

1 Cut Da Carb wrap

2 tsp. mustard (8 g)

2 tsp. honey mustard (8 g)

1 slice light Swiss cheese (21 g)

3 slices Canadian bacon or ham (I use Costco's Canadian bacon)

1 small tomato, sliced (75 g)

Red onion, thinly sliced (15 g)

1 oz pepperoncinis (banana peppers)

1-2 Tbsp. jarred pickled sweet cherry peppers (or roasted red peppers)

Butter lettuce, chopped

Red wine vinegar + salt and pepper

1 oz (28 g) lite Italian dry salami (I use Columbus brand)

Search MFP for: "Lillie Eats and Tells Italian Stallion Crunch Wrap Naked." This will show you lower macros withOUT the wrap, so you can log this filling ALONG with whatever wrap you use.

Macros with the Cut Da Carb:
310 Cal, 9F, 25C, 31P, 7 Fiber

1. Build wrap by spreading mustards in the middle. Top with Swiss, Canadian bacon or ham, tomato slices, onions, pepperoncinis, sweet cherry peppers, and lettuce. Drizzle with a little red wine vinegar (careful not to get the wrap wet and soggy) and sprinkle with salt and pepper. Top with salami (this helps protect the lettuce from getting too much heat).

2. Crunch wrap it.

EASY FIG AND GOAT CHEESE CHICKEN BURGER CRUNCH WRAP

Inspired by my all-time favorite burger from Eureka Burger®, this is an extra quick, easy, and LIGHT version made with a store-bought burger. A homemade turkey-burger version can be found on my blog (lillieeatsandtells.com).

1 Cut Da Carb wrap

2 tsp. (10 g) Fig Butter (Trader Joe's) or other sweet preserve

1.5 Tbsp. skinny chipotle cream (20 g) (see "flavor makers")

1 Don Lee Farms Chicken Patty®**

½ oz (14 g) honey goat cheese chevre (I love the one at Trader Joe's)

1 Tbsp. (15 g) caramelized onion**

Pinch of raw, red onion

Handful of arugula

1 piece of bacon

¼ of a small avocado (20 g)

Search MFP for: "Lillie Eats and Tells Easy Fig and Goat Cheese Chicken Burger Crunch Wrap Naked." This will show you lower macros withOUT the wrap, so you can log this filling ALONG with whatever wrap you use.

Macros with the Cut Da Carb:
387 Cal, 12F, 36C, 32P, 9 Fiber

1. Spread wrap with fig butter and skinny chipotle cream. Top with chicken burger (not too hot to avoid tearing the wrap).

2. Spread burger with goat cheese. Then top with caramelized onion, extra red onion (if adding), arugula, bacon, and avocado.

3. Crunch wrap it!

*We get these burgers at Costco, and I love them for a super easy dinner option. They've got that lean, store-bought burger texture, but the macros are amazing (2c/2.5f/20p), and the flavor is so good! My whole family loves them. But use whatever burger you like, of course.

** Cook thinly sliced onion over medium heat with cooking spray and salt for 15-20 minutes until soft and caramelized. Store and use on everything!

FRESH THAI CHICKEN CRUNCH WRAP

Because you finally found this delicious Thai Coconut Curry Hummus and want to find places to put it all day.

1 Cut Da Carb wrap

2 Tbsp. Hope Foods® Thai Coconut Curry Hummus (or regular hummus with a pinch of curry powder mixed in)

3.5 oz (100 g) favorite deli chicken or rotisserie chicken

¼ of a small avocado (20 g)

Mango, sliced thin (30 g)

Bell pepper, diced (20 g)

Cucumber, sliced (30 g)

Shredded cabbage (80 g)

1 Tbsp. Trader Joe's Spicy Peanut Vinaigrette (or other favorite Asian dressing)*

*Newman's Own® Sesame Ginger is another good, light, store-bought option.

1. Spread hummus in the middle of the wrap.

2. Top with 50 g of the chicken, avocado, mango, bell pepper, cucumber, and cabbage.

3. Drizzle with dressing and top with additional 50 g of chicken.

4. Crunch wrap it.

Search MFP for: "Lillie Eats and Tells Fresh Thai Chicken Crunch Wrap Naked." This will show you lower macros withOUT the wrap, so you can log this filling ALONG with whatever wrap you use.

Macros with the Cut Da Carb:
351 Cal, 11F, 35C, 29P, 10 Fiber

DIPPY CHICKEN PARMESAN CRUNCH WRAP

1 Cut Da Carb wrap

1 Tbsp. light basil, garlic aioli (15 g) (see "flavor makers")

2 Tbsp. part-skim ricotta (30 g) mixed with ¼ clove of minced garlic (or just a little!)

3.5 oz skinless rotisserie chicken breast (100 g)

A pinch of shaved parmesan (10 g)

Handful of arugula

Small handful of fresh, torn basil

1/4 cup marinara for dipping (my favorite is Victoria Organic® from Costco)

About 1 tsp (5 g) balsamic glaze

Search MFP for: "Lillie Eats and Tells Dippy Chicken Parmesan Crunch Wrap Naked." This will show you lower macros withOUT the wrap, so you can log this filling ALONG with whatever wrap you use.

Macros with the Cut Da Carb:
345 Cal, 9F, 23C, 39P, 6 Fiber

1. Thaw cubes of garlic if using and mix all aioli ingredients together.

2. In the middle of your wrap, spread basil aioli, then garlicky ricotta mixture. Top with shredded chicken (seasoned with a little salt and garlic if not already seasoned), balsamic glaze, parmesan, basil, and a little arugula.

3. Crunch wrap it. Serve with marinara for dipping and a little extra balsamic glaze.

This is also delicious made with the Tyson® Panko Breaded Chicken Breast Tenderloins from Costco!

EASY MAHI BURGER CRUNCH WRAP

Another super easy option when I don't have a homemade protein on hand. Or just because I LOVE these mahi burgers! I'm a huge salmon fan, but I much prefer these to any store-bought salmon burger I've found.

1 Cut Da Carb wrap

1 Spicy Pepper Jack Laughing Cow Cheese wedge

1 Trader Joe's Mahi Burger (or other favorite fish burger)

1 Tbsp. fat-free sour cream mixed with 5 grams sriracha (if you can only find reduced fat, it will hardly make a difference in the macros!)

1 small Roma tomatoes, sliced thick (90 g)

¼ of an avocado (28 g)

Pinch of red onion (15 g)

Pinch of sweet bell pepper, chopped (15 g)

Handful of shredded cabbage, green or purple (tossed in a little vinegar or lime)*

Cilantro

*You can use the cabbage dry, but I like to toss mine in a little something acidic first to make it more of a slaw. If you've got any Cilantro-Lime Slaw from the Lillie Eats and Tells Cookbook or blog, that's the best!

Search MFP for: "Lillie Eats and Tells Easy Mahi Burger Crunch Wrap Naked." This will show you lower macros withOUT the wrap, so you can log this filling ALONG with whatever wrap you use.

Macros with the Cut Da Carb:
312 Cal, 12F, 26C, 24P, 9 Fiber

1. Spread center of flatbread with cheese wedge. Top with slightly cooled, pan-seared mahi burger, tomatoes, avocado, red onion, bell peppers, cabbage and cilantro!

2. Crunch wrap it!

WEEK NIGHT CRUNCH WRAPS

The perfect, light and healthy dinner to throw together using some homemade, bulk-prepared protein you might have lying around for the week!

CUBANO
CHICAGO TURKEY BURGER
GREEK CHICKEN
TACO
BLISTERED TOMATO BASIL
FAJITA CHICKEN
ITAILAN MEATBALL
BBQ PULLED PORK
SHREDDED CHICKEN TOSTADA
BUFFALO CHICKEN
PORK TENDERLOIN, SMASHED SWEET POTATO

CUBANO CRUNCH WRAP

What you have for lunch the day after you prepared the 10-Minute Skinny Cuban Sandwich or Greek Pork Pitas for the fam! (Both in the Lillie Eats and Tells Cookbook.) You won't even miss the bread.

1 Cut Da Carb wrap

1 Spicy Pepper Jack Laughing Cow Cheese wedge

1 Tbsp. creamy chimichurri (see "flavor makers")

1 slice (21g) reduced-fat Swiss cheese

3 oz (80 g) Instant Pot Shredded Greek Pork or Salsa Verde Crispy Carintas (from the Lillie Eats and Tells Cookbook)

1 Tbsp. caramelized onions (15g)(sauté in a pan with salt, med-low heat until soft)*

½ oz pepperoncinis (15 g)

2 tsp. (8 g) honey mustard (I just use French's brand)

Yellow mustard (however much you like)

Arugula

Fresh mint

2 slices Trader Joe's Healthy Ham or favorite lean ham (0F/10P for the TJ)

Search MFP for: "Lillie Eats and Tells Cubano Crunch Wrap Naked." This will show you lower macros withOUT the wrap, so you can log this filling ALONG with whatever wrap you use.

Macros with the Cut Da Carb:
366 Cal, 6F, 26C, 41P, 7 Fiber

1. Build wrap by spreading Laughing Cow wedge, then creamy chimichurri, Swiss, pork, onions (raw or pickled are great, too!), pepperoncinis, mustards, arugula, fresh mint if using, and end with ham.

2. Crunch wrap it!

A quick, yummy substitute for the creamy chimichurri is the Green Goddess dressing from Trader Joe's.

* Onions usually shrink in half when they are soft and caramelized. So if you were cooking just your portion, you'd cook 30 g raw onion to produce 15 g caramelized onion. Or you can sauté as much as you like and save for later! If you're logging them for other meals, just log raw onions, but log twice as much as you take of the cooked onion. Pile 10 grams of caramlized onion on a burger and log 20 g raw onion.

CHICAGO TURKEY BURGER
CRUNCH WRAP

Inspired by my favorite hot dog that blew me away because I never would have guessed I'd love it! This is not my classic flavor profile, but I'm tell-ing you, there's something about it! Unless you hate mustard and pickles like I do olives, don't write it off. Even though it's not that photogenic, bless its heart.

1 Cut Da Carb wrap

2 tsp. mustard (mixed with 2 tsp. fat-free sour cream if you like the creami-ness)

1 Tbsp. sweet relish (15 g)

4 oz turkey burger (explained in step 1 but leftovers work great!)

1 small tomato, sliced thick (90 g)

Red or white onion, sliced thin (20 g) (I did pickled!)

Pickles

1 oz Pepperoncinis

Celery salt

Crunchy lettuce like Romaine or ice-berg

Search MFP for: "Lillie Eats and Tells Chi-cago Turkey Burger Crunch Wrap Naked." This will show you lower macros withOUT the wrap, so you can log this filling ALONG with whatever wrap you use.

Macros with the Cut Da Carb:
292 Cal, 27C, 9F, 27P, 7 Fiber

1. Form raw 93/7 ground turkey into 4-oz balls. Place on a large plate or surface and carefully smash until nice and flat. Season generously with kosher or coarse salt, a pinch of pepper, and a sprinkle of garlic powder on each side. (I season the second side while the first side is cooking.) Cook burgers in a skillet with cooking spray over pretty high heat for 2-3 minutes per side.

2. Build wrap by spreading mustard mixture and relish in the middle. Then top with just slightly warm turkey burger, tomato, onion, pickles, pepper-oncinis, celery salt, and lettuce.

3. Crunch wrap it.

GREEK CHICKEN CRUNCH WRAP

This is the crunch wrap you make for lunch the day after you've cooked the Mediterranean Arugula and Grain Bowl or Greek Pork Pitas (both in my Lillie Eats and Tells Cookbook) for your family! Because you are not going to want to let that cucumber salsa go to waste.

1 Cut Da Carb wrap

2 Tbsp. (30 g) of a lower-fat hummus (I like Hope Hummus®, 2.5/serving)

3 oz (80 g) grilled Greek chicken from the Lillie Eats and Tells Cookbook or whatever chicken you have!*

½ cup (100 g) Greek salsa (recipe below)

2 Tbsp. (30 g) tzatziki (Trader Joe's has a great one!)

Handful of arugula

1 Tbsp. (15 g) pickled red onion (see "flavor makers")

Pickled cabbage(10 g)* (just throw shredded cabbage in with a batch of onions)

Squeeze of lemon

FOR THE GREEK SALSA
(Serves about 8)

2 cups of cucumber, diced (250 g)

2 cups firm, Roma tomatoes, diced (250 g)

1 small red onion, diced (150 g)

1 cup red bell pepper, diced (120 g)

1 Tbsp. olive oil

1/4 cup fat-free feta

1/4 -1/2 cup fresh mint, depending on taste

Big pinch or two of kosher salt

Fresh ground pepper to taste

Juice from 1 lemon

1. Make Greek salsa by tossing all of the salsa ingredients together. It will get more watery over time, but we still love it for 3-4 days out of the fridge.

2. Lay wrap flat. In the center, spread the hummus, then top with chicken, cucumber salsa, arugula, a drizzle of tzatziki, pickled onions, and cabbage. Squeeze with lemon.

3. Crunch wrap it.

Search MFP for: "Lillie Eats and Tells Greek Chicken Crunch Wrap Naked." This will show you lower macros withOUT the wrap, so you can log this filling ALONG with whatever wrap you use.

Macros with the Cut Da Carb:
302 Cal, 7F, 29C, 29P, 8 Fiber

TACO CRUNCH WRAP

Lunch the day after any Mexican food spread. Of course.

1 Cut Da Carb wrap

1 Spicy Pepper Jack Laughing Cow Cheese wedge

1.5 Tbsp. (20 g) skinny chipotle cream (see "flavor makers")

3.5 oz cooked extra-lean ground turkey seasoned for tacos (100 g cooked)

Chopped lettuce

Mango, sliced thin (30 g)

Bell pepper, diced (20 g)

Avocado, sliced thin (20 g)

¼ cup pico de gallo (60 g) (storebought or see recipe in the Lillie Eats and Tells Cookbook)

1 Tbsp. homemade cilantro-lime ranch (15 g) (see "flavor makers")

Fresh cilantro

Search MFP for: "Lillie Eats and Tells Taco Crunch Wrap Naked." This will show you lower macros withOUT the wrap, so you can log this filling ALONG with whatever wrap you use.

Macros with the Cut Da Carb:
324 Cal, 33C, 7F, 31P, 8 Fiber

1. Build wrap by spreading Laughing Cow wedge, chipotle cream, half the meat (cool to avoid a soggy wrap), lettuce, mango, bell pepper, avocado, pico, dressing, and the other half of the meat. (I like this technique to protect the veggies from the heat.)

2. Crunch wrap it.

BLISTERED TOMATO BASIL CRUNCH WRAP

This one is on my blog (lillieeatsandtells.com) and is inspired by the Roasted Tomato Basil Chicken Sandwich (in the Lillie Eats and Tells Cookbook and also on my blog.) A quick and easy way to get those restaurant-quality flavors!

1 Cut Da Carb wrap

2-3 Tbsp. marinara sauce

1 wedge Spicy Pepper Jack Laughing Cow cheese

15 g quick basil, garlic aioli (see "flavor makers")

3.5 oz (100 g) grilled chicken

Handful of cherry tomatoes (70 g)

A sprinkle of garlic powder, salt, and pepper

A few fresh basil leaves, torn

Handful of arugula

Search MFP for: "Lillie Eats and Tells Blistered Tomato Basil Crunch Wrap Naked." This will show you lower macros withOUT the wrap, so you can log this filling ALONG with whatever wrap you use.

Macros with the Cut Da Carb:
318 Cal, 27C, 6F, 35P, 8 Fiber

1. Heat a non-stick pan to med-high heat and throw in halved tomatoes with cooking spray, a sprinkle of kosher salt, pepper, and garlic powder. Let them cook for a minute or so.

2. Throw your chicken in the other half of the same pan, also spraying and seasoning. Leave on FOR JUST A MINUTE, flipping and tossing a little. Don't go crazy—we don't want gross, reheated poultry. Just enough to warm and season, and maybe get a crispy bit here and there.

3. Remove tomatoes and chicken from the pan and turn the pan off (or on low) while you build your wrap. You'll want the pan hot again when you're ready to cook your wrap.

4. Now build your wrap (on a plate, on your scale, if you count your macros). Spread the Laughing Cow wedge in a circle around the middle of your wrap, then add the basil aioli, chicken, tomatoes, marinara, basil, and arugula. (Remember to zero out your scale between each addition.)

5. Crunch wrap it.

FAJITA CHICKEN CRUNCH WRAP

Because you had fajitas last night for dinner!

1 Cut Da Carb wrap

1 oz light pepper jack cheese (3 fat)

3.5 oz (100 g) fajita chicken*

1 Tbsp. (15 g) fat-free sour cream

2 Tbsp. favorite salsa (I love the double roasted from Trader Joe's)

¼ cup (60 g) sautéed bell peppers and onions*

¼ of an avocado (25 g)

3-4 slices (70 g) tomato

Large pinch of cilantro

Arugula for more green (optional)

* The macros are calculated with the Fajita Chicken and Veggies I have on my blog (lillieeatsandtells.com). You can search them there, or just sauté your chicken and veggies in a pan with whatever fajita seasonings you like. If you don't add oil, our macros will be essentially the same!

Search MFP for: "Lillie Eats and Tells Fajita Chicken Crunch Wrap Naked." This will show you lower macros withOUT the wrap, so you can log this filling ALONG with whatever wrap you use.

Macros with the Cut Da Carb:
431 Cal, 10F, 34C, 48P, 9 Fiber

1. Lay one slice of light pepper jack in the center of the wrap.

2. Top with chicken, sour cream, salsa, veggies, avocado, tomatoes, cilantro, and arugula if using.

3. Crunch wrap it.

4. Eat it with some creamy cilantro-lime ranch or jalapeño avocado dressing! (Both found in "flavor makers.")

ITALIAN MEATBALL CRUNCH WRAP

Lunch the day after your family ate the Classic Meatball Sub from the Lillie Eats and Tells Cookbook! These turkey-mushroom meatballs are a favorite protein of mine to prep ahead and use in a number of ways. They can only be found in the cookbook, but feel free to use any meatballs and adjust the macros accordingly! I've got two other light meatball options on my blog (lillieeatsandtells.com).

1 Cut Da Carb wrap

2 Tbsp. (25 g) light basil, garlic aioli (see "flavor makers")

1 slice lite provolone cheese (3 fat for mine)

150 g Turkey-Mushroom Meatballs (from the Lillie Eats and Tells Cookbook) or other favorite meatball

3-4 Tbsp. marinara (I love Victoria Organic from Costco)

Handful of arugula

1 small tomato sliced (90 g)

Pinch of red onion, sliced thinly (15 g)

Search MFP for: "Lillie Eats and Tells Italian Meatball Crunch Wrap Naked." This will show you lower macros withOUT the wrap, so you can log this filling ALONG with whatever wrap you use.

Macros with the Cut Da Carb:
343 Cal, 6F, 33C, 38P, 8 Fiber

1. Spread middle of flatbread with basil garlic aioli. Top with cheese, meatballs, marinara, arugula, tomatoes, and onion.

2. Crunch wrap it!

BBQ PULLED-PORK
CRUNCH WRAP with CILANTRO-LIME SLAW

This is the crunch wrap you make for lunch the day after you've prepared the Lightened-up, BBQ Pulled-Pork Sandwich (from the Lillie Eats and Tells Cookbook) for dinner!

1 Cut Da Carb wrap

1 Spicy Pepper Jack Laughing Cow Cheese wedge

Small handful of fresh cilantro

5+ oz (150 g) pulled pork*

1 Tbsp. Stubb's BBQ Sauce®

Handful of shredded cabbage (60-100 g) tossed in vinegar or lime juice**

Bell pepper, diced (20 g)

Handful of arugula

*Macros are calculated with the BBQ Pulled Pork from the Lillie Eats and Tells Cookbook, but use whatever lean pulled pork you have; it will be very similar as long as it's not cooked in fat or sugar. If you don't have the cookbook, the recipe is also on my blog, lillieeatsandtells.com. You can search for it there!

** If you've got leftover Cilantro-Lime Slaw from your pulled-pork sandwiches in the cookbook, use that! Macros for 100 grams will be almost the same as plain cabbage.

Search MFP for: "Lillie Eats and Tells BBQ Pulled-Pork Crunch Wrap Naked." This will show you lower macros withOUT the wrap, so you can log this filling ALONG with whatever wrap you use.

Macros with the Cut Da Carb:
343 Cal, 4F, 31C, 37P, 8 Fiber

1. Spread cheese wedge in center of wrap, top with cilantro, slightly cooled pulled pork, BBQ sauce, slaw, diced bell pepper, and arugula.

2. Crunch wrap it!

SHREDDED CHICKEN TOSTADA CRUNCH WRAP

Because we have to have at least one wrap with the actual "crunch" inside like Taco Bell.

1 Cut Da Carb wrap

1.5 Tbsp. fat-free sour cream (20 g) (reduced fat won't change the macros much!)

3.5 oz shredded chicken (100 g)(season with taco seasoning if it's not already seasoned)

1 Extra-thin Mission Corn Tortilla® (pan fried 'til crispy. See step 1.)

2 Tbsp. fat-free refried beans (30 g)

1.5 Tbsp. avocado, thinly sliced (20 g)

Chopped lettuce

2 Tbsp. jarred queso (Trader Joe's is the one I use for these macros, but use whatever you have!)

2 tsp. cotija cheese (10 g)

¼ cup pico (60 g) (store-bought, or see Lillie Eats and Tells Cookbook for a recipe)

Fresh cilantro

1 Tbsp. Creamy Jalapeño Avocado Dressing (15 g) (see "flavor makers")

Search MFP for: "Lillie Eats and Tells Shredded Chicken Tostada Crunch Wrap Naked." This will show you lower macros withOUT the wrap, so you can log this filling ALONG with whatever wrap you use.

Macros with the Cut Da Carb:
396 Cal, 7F, 42C, 39P, 10 Fiber

1. Cook tortilla in pan over medium-high heat with a little cooking spray and salt, for a few minutes per side, until crispy. You can do this ahead and keep in a sealed container.

2. Build wrap by spreading sour cream in the middle of Cut Da Carb. Top with chicken. Place homemade tostada (fried tortilla) on top of chicken and spread with refried beans and avocado. Top with lettuce, drizzle with queso, and sprinkle with cotija cheese. Finish with pico, Creamy Jalapeño Avocado Dressing, and extra cilantro.

3. Crunch wrap it.

BUFFALO CHICKEN
CRUNCH WRAP

A delicious home for your leftover Creamy Buffalo Chicken (from the Lillie Eats and Tells Cookbook), but any shredded chicken will work just fine!

1 Cut Da Carb wrap

1 Spicy Pepper Jack Laughing Cow Cheese wedge

1 Tbsp. Bolthouse® Ranch

3 oz (80 g) shredded chicken (use leftover Creamy Buffalo Chicken from the Lillie Eats and Tells Cookbook if you have it!)

Butter lettuce (or Romaine or iceberg)

¼ a small avocado (20 g)

Pinch of reduced-fat blue cheese (6 g)*

1 small tomato, sliced (90 g)

Pinch of pickled onion (25 g) (see "flavor makers")

Diced sweet bell pepper (20 g)

Frank's RedHot® Buffalo Sauce to taste

* If you can't find reduced-fat blue cheese (I buy the Treasure Cave® brand), just use regular! A little goes a long way and doesn't add a ton of fat.

Search MFP for: "Lillie Eats and Tells Buffalo Chicken Crunch Wrap Naked." This will show you lower macros withOUT the wrap, so you can log this filling ALONG with whatever wrap you use.

Macros with the Cut Da Carb:
314 Cal, 10F, 28C, 26P, 9 Fiber

1. Build wrap by spreading Laughing Cow wedge, then ranch, half the chicken, lettuce, thinly sliced avocado, blue cheese, tomatoes, pickled onions, bell pepper, a little additional hot sauce, and the rest of the chicken.

2. Crunch wrap it. Be careful because this one will be juicy if you're using buffalo chicken. If you don't like the juiciness, you can heat the chicken in a pan before to dry it out it a bit.

PORK TENDERLOIN, SMASHED SWEET POTATO CRUNCH WRAP WITH CREAMY CHIMICHURRI

Otherwise known as "Monday's Crunch Wrap," since we love to grill pork tenderloin on Sundays!

1 Cut da Carb wrap

1 Spicy Pepper Jack Laughing Cow Cheese wedge

1.5 Tbsp. creamy chimichurri (20 g) (see "flavor makers")

A few slices (40 g) of baked sweet potato

3 oz (80 g) leftover Brown Sugar Spiced Pork Tenderloin (on my blog, lillieeatsandtells.com) or any pork tenderloin

1 small Roma tomato, sliced thin (80 g)

Pinch of pickled red onion (15 g) (see "flavor makers")

¼ of a small avocado, sliced thin (20 g)

Fresh jalapeno, serrano, or sweet bell peppers, diced (20 g)

Handful of arugula

1. Spread middle of wrap with cheese wedge, then 20 g creamy chimichurri.

2. Smash baked sweet potato on to the wrap, then top with half of the sliced pork tenderloin, followed by tomatoes, pickled onions, avocado, jalapenos, and arugula. Top with remaining pork.

3. Crunch wrap it!

Search MFP for: "Lillie Eats and Tells Pork Tenderloin Smashed Sweet Potato Crunch Wrap Naked." This will show you lower macros withOUT the wrap, so you can log this filling ALONG with whatever wrap you use.

Macros with the Cut Da Carb:
383 Cal, 9F, 42C, 32P, 10 Fiber

MIDNIGHT MUNCH WRAPS

BERRIES AND CREAM COBBLER
APPLE PIE, CREAM CHEESE

BERRIES AND CREAM COBBLER CRUNCH WRAP

Okay, this one is definitely a "fork-and-knife" crunch wrap. But it's worth it.

1 Cut Da Carb wrap

1 Tbsp. whipped Greek cream cheese

1 cup frozen mixed berries

1-2 droppers or packets of Stevia

½ tsp. almond extract (or sub vanilla)

¼ tsp. cinnamon

1 Tbsp. fresh-squeezed lemon juice

½ cup (119g) low-fat cottage cheese (Knudsen® is my all-time favorite)

Sprinkle of powdered sugar (3 g)

Search MFP for: "Lillie Eats and Tells Berries and Cream Cobbler Crunch Wrap Naked." This will show you lower macros withOUT the wrap, so you can log this filling ALONG with whatever wrap you use.

Macros with the Cut Da Carb:
264 Cal, 4F, 37C, 17P, 10 Fiber

1. Toss frozen berries with Stevia, almond extract, cinnamon, and lemon juice. Stir in cottage cheese. It'll be nice and cold and THAT'S GOOD.

2. Spread wrap with Greek cream cheese, top with berry and cottage cheese mixture.

3. Crunch wrap it.

4. Sprinkle with powdered sugar, top with yogurt (or ice cream), and enjoy!

APPLE PIE, CREAM CHEESE CRUNCH WRAP

I'll let you decide if you eat this as a light, hand-held breakfast, paired with yogurt for a healthy afternoon snack, or smothered in ice cream like PIE. We prefer the last option! (Remember, this is not actually buttery pie dough, so it's not going to flake away with each bite. But, it is delicious!)

1 Cut Da Carb wrap

1 large Granny Smith apple, thinly sliced (125 g)

A squeeze of fresh lemon (about 1 Tbsp.)

2 packets of Stevia

¼ tsp. cinnamon

Light sprinkle of cloves and nutmeg

2 Tbsp. (22 g) whipped Greek creamcheese (2c/2.5f/3p). If you can't find this, sub reduced-fat cream cheese for just a small difference in macros.

1. Toss apple slices in lemon juice, Stevia, cinnamon, cloves, and a little nutmeg.

2. Heat a pan over medium heat and spray with cooking spray. Add the apples and sauté for about 3-5 minutes or until tender. Remove from pan and let cool for a minute.

3. Spread middle of wrap with Greek cream cheese sprinkled with a little extra Stevia. Top with sautéed apples.

4. Crunch wrap it.

5. Sprinkle with cinnamon. Top with Two Good® yogurt to add pretty much just protein, or top with your favorite lighter ice cream.

Search MFP for: "Lillie Eats and Tells Apple Pie, Cream Cheese Crunch Wrap Naked." This will show you lower macros withOUT the wrap, so you can log this filling ALONG with whatever wrap you use.

Macros with the Cut Da Carb:
198 Cal, 3F, 33C, 7P, 8 Fiber

Thank you to my friend, Jarica Watts,
for helping me edit this book!

AND THANK YOU FOR YOUR SUPPORT.
I HOPE YOU KEEP IN TOUCH:

www.lillieeatsandtells.com
Instagram: @lillieeatsandtells
Facebook: Lillie Eats and Tells

I'd love to see your creations on Instagram!
Tag me @lillieeatsandtells and hashtag #LEATcrunchwrap
when you're sitting down to your favorite lunches ever.

xo Lillie